Carol Lerner

Plants that make you Sniffle and Sneeze

Morrow Junior Books
New York

FIREWEED

The author thanks Professor Walter H. Lewis of Washington University, St. Louis, for reviewing the manuscript.

Watercolors were used for the full-color artwork.
The text type is 14-point Bembo.

Printed in Hong Kong by South China Printing Company (1988) Ltd.
1   2   3   4   5   6   7   8   9   10

Library of Congress Cataloging-in-Publication Data
Lerner, Carol.
    Plants that make you sniffle and sneeze / Carol Lerner.
        p.   cm.
    Includes bibliographical references and index.
    Summary: Discusses hay fever and describes the various plants
whose pollen triggers hay fever allergies, with information on where
they grow, how their pollen is dispersed, and what can be done to
avoid exposure to these irritants.
    ISBN 0-688-11489-X (trade). — ISBN 0-688-11490-3 (library)
    1. Hay fever—Juvenile literature. [1. Hay fever.   2. Allergy.]
I. Title.
RC590.L47   1993
616.2'02—dc20   92-21561   CIP   AC

CONTENTS

INTRODUCTION

Allergies are as old as human history. From ancient times there have been people who become sick whenever they eat milk products or eggs. Millions of people also suffer because they are sensitive to something in the air they breathe. The unseen cause of their misery might be dust, molds, tiny flakes of skin from the family cat, or hundreds of other things. Any substance that sets off an allergic reaction is called an allergen.

If the allergic symptoms come and go at the same time each year, the allergen is likely to be grains of plant pollen carried in the air. We call this kind of sickness hay fever, though it isn't caused by hay and it doesn't make a person's body temperature rise.

Until the nineteenth century the cause of hay fever was a mystery. Some people thought that high summer temperatures set off their illness. Others blamed the odors of certain flowers and herbs. Charles Blackley, an English researcher who suffered from hay fever, tested these theories by performing hundreds of experiments on himself. In 1873 he published his results, showing that plant pollen was the cause of his symptoms.

Hay fever is the most common of all allergic diseases, affecting from ten to twenty percent of the population in the United States. A hay fever sufferer usually has the same symptoms as someone sick with a cold—runny nose and eyes and lots of sneezing. Some people have trouble breathing.

Hay fever runs in families. A child who has one parent with hay fever has a fifty-fifty chance of developing it. If both parents have hay fever, the likelihood is seventy-five to eighty percent. But the allergy doesn't begin to show up until after repeated exposures to the allergenic material. Symptoms often start to appear between the ages of five and ten years. Some children outgrow their hay fever by the time they become young adults, and some people develop pollen allergies only in their adult years.

There is no practical way to escape from all the plants that may cause hay fever. No part of the country is completely free of them. They grow in forests, fields, suburbs, and cities.

People can be tested to discover which plants trigger their allergies. Doctors can provide treatment and medicines that control the symptoms and make the patient more comfortable, but they cannot cure the condition.

Hay fever victims can do some things to help themselves, however. Their best defense is to avoid receiving large doses of the allergens that affect them. But to do that they must know something about the sources of those pollens.

This book looks at plants that scatter their pollens into the air and at the conditions that set off pollen release. It describes the groups of hay fever plants that are shedding pollen as the calendar moves from spring to fall. And it points out some of the most troublesome plants that flower at each stage in the growing season. Because of climate and temperature differences between Texas and Maine, or between Oregon and New York, flowering times for each species vary widely in different parts of the continent. Local and regional field guides will provide precise dates.

ONE

POLLEN IN THE AIR

We seldom notice plant pollen. A single grain of pollen is just a speck, too small to see without the help of a microscope. Yet every plant that makes seeds produces pollen at some time in the growing season—every tree and bush, weed and garden flower, grass, and each one of the plants growing in farmers' fields. And many plants produce pollen in huge amounts. Hundreds of millions of the tiny grains may come from a single flowering bush.

The word *pollen* comes from a Latin root and means "fine flour" or "dust." Different kinds of plants produce pollen grains in a wide range of sizes, but the grains are always small—so small that their size is measured in microns. (A micron is one thousandth of a millimeter.)

One of the largest pollen grains comes from the flower of a pumpkin plant and measures around two hundred microns in diameter. A forget-me-not pollen, about four and one-half microns, is among the smallest. Two hundred and twenty grains of forget-me-not pollen, stacked end to end, would form a line about one millimeter long.

Pollen grains develop in a plant's stamens, which are the male parts of a flower. Typically, stamens have threadlike stalks and grow in a circle around the flower's center. Each stamen is topped by an anther, usually yellow, containing the pollen.

The female part of a typical flower, the pistil, grows at the blossom's center inside the ring of stamens. At its tip is the stigma, which is usually sticky. The lower part of the pistil contains the ovary. This is where the plant's seeds grow.

THE PARTS OF A TYPICAL FLOWER

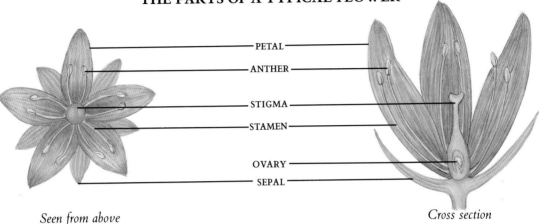

PETAL
ANTHER
STIGMA
STAMEN
OVARY
SEPAL

Seen from above

Cross section

A ring of bright petals surrounds the male and female flower parts. Beneath them are the green sepals that wrapped and protected the flower until it opened.

Before a flower can develop fruit and seeds, it must be pollinated—that is, pollen from some plant of the same species must be placed on its stigma. The typical flower described here is probably pollinated by a bee or some other insect. Its colorful petals send a long-distance signal to animal pollinators. The flower may also have a strong odor to advertise its presence.

Insects, of course, are not interested in flowers because of their beauty or their perfume. They come to eat the nourishing pollen. Some flowers also offer them sips of sweet liquid nectar from special glands deep within the blossom.

As an insect feasts, its body brushes against the stamens and picks up a dusting of pollen. When it flies off to feed at the next flower, some of the pollen may rub off on the second flower's stigma and stick to it. In time, male cells in the pollen grain join with the female cells in the ovary. If the pollen came from a plant of the same species, the ovary will produce fruit and seeds after this union.

Insect pollinators move systematically from flower to flower, from plant to plant. Pollen from one plant often ends up on the pistil of another. This mixing between different plants of the same species is called cross-pollination.

Plants that grow from cross-pollinated seeds are a little different from the parent plants because they combine qualities from both of them. Some of the plants resulting from the mixture may be stronger or better adapted to the habitat. In the long run, the ability to change is an advantage to plants.

The great majority of plant species depend on some kind of insect, bird, or bat to distribute their pollen. But there are exceptions: The pollen of some plants is spread by wind.

These flowers look very different from the blossoms of insect-pollinated plants. They are small—in fact, you may need a magnifying glass to get a good look at them. Wind-pollinated flowers are often green and their colors dull. They usually have only the essential flower parts—male stamens and female pistils. They have no need for large, bright petals to attract animals, so they are usually petal-less. Instead of green sepals, they may have only small scalelike bracts to cover the tiny flower parts before they open. There is no store of sugary nectar and no perfume to lure visitors.

In many insect-pollinated flowers, the stamens and pistils are protected by the other flower parts. They are often tightly enclosed within joined and folded petals, forcing the feeding insect to push its way into the flower's center. In contrast, the anthers and stigmas of wind-pollinated flowers must be fully exposed to wind currents. Their stamens often dangle in the air, sometimes in long swinging catkins like those of the poplar tree. Their pistils have large, sticky stigmas. Many of these stigmas are feathery or comblike, making it easier to snag the tiny grains of pollen as they float by on the breeze.

Many wind-pollinated flowers are even further simplified. Wind-pollinated plants commonly have two different kinds of flowers—one kind

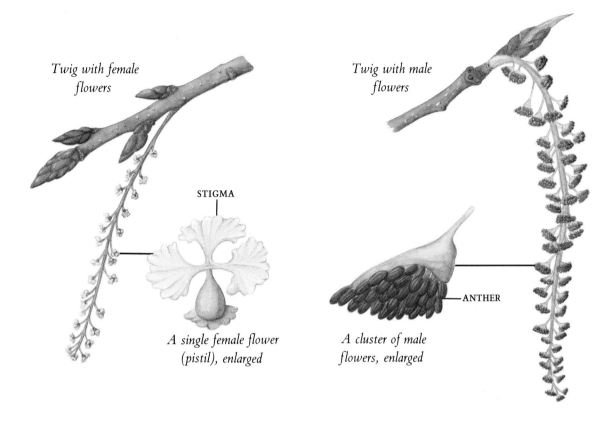

Twig with female flowers

STIGMA

A single female flower (pistil), enlarged

Twig with male flowers

ANTHER

A cluster of male flowers, enlarged

with stamens but no pistils, and the other with pistils alone. In some species these single-sex flowers grow on the same plant. In others, they grow separately. A poplar tree, for example, has male flowers or female flowers, but not both. Having stamens and pistils on separate plants guarantees cross-pollination.

Species with male and female parts on the same plants usually have some barrier to prevent pollination by their own anthers. An example is English plantain, a common weed. Plantain bears many tiny flowers on an upright spike. Each flower has both male and female parts, but they mature at different times. First the stigma emerges from the still-closed flower. By the time the flower opens and the stamens come out, the stigma on that flower has already been fertilized by pollen from another plantain.

Wind pollination is not a dependable delivery system. The chance that

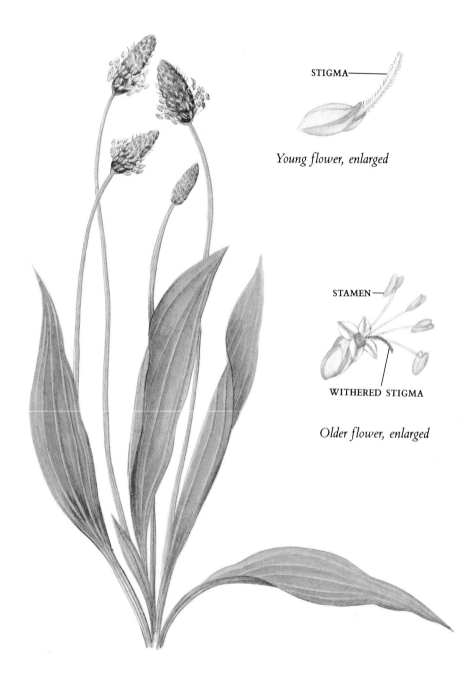

STIGMA

Young flower, enlarged

STAMEN

WITHERED STIGMA

Older flower, enlarged

ENGLISH PLANTAIN WITH FLOWERS

any single grain of poplar pollen will land on a poplar stigma is very small. Most wind-borne pollen settles on leaves and branches, on the flowers of other species, on houses and cars, and on the ground. Thousands are lost for one that reaches its goal.

The wind-pollinated plants survive because they produce huge quantities of pollen, usually far more than the insect-pollinated plants do. When pollen pours from their anthers, the air around them is filled with powder. So, in spite of the great loss, enough pollen lands on target to guarantee a new generation of plants.

The pollen of wind-pollinated plants is not only more abundant than that of insect-pollinated species but it also differs in size, appearance, and stickiness.

In order to be carried in the air, grains must be lightweight. Most wind-borne pollen is very small, between twenty and forty microns in diameter. Grains smaller than that are not good floaters, probably because they have a tendency to stick together in clumps.

POLLEN GRAINS,
MUCH ENLARGED

*A wind-borne pollen
(English plantain)*

*An insect-carried pollen
(annual sunflower)*

Each kind of plant has its characteristic pollen. Grains vary in shape as well as size and also in the pattern of furrows, pores, ridges, or spines on the outer layer. This surface sculpturing makes it possible to look at a speck of pollen and identify the plant or plant group from which it came. It is not always possible to know the exact species because pollen from closely related plants may look alike.

The outer layer of an airborne pollen is usually thin and smooth. In contrast, insect-borne pollens have a thick skin that is heavily sculptured. More important, pollen from flowers visited by insects is usually covered by an oily coating. The grains cling to one another and to anything that touches the anther. After feeding on the flower, an insect's body is likely to be covered by bundles of sticky pollen. This is no great burden for the insect, but such bundles are too heavy to float on the wind. Airborne pollen, however, is usually dry on the outside, allowing individual grains to separate easily and blow from the plant one at a time, or in twos and threes.

After leaving the anther, pollen is easily spoiled by moisture. If it is soaked by raindrops or if the humidity is high, it loses its power to fertilize a stigma. Rain also, of course, washes floating pollen out of the air.

Flower anthers remain closed in cold and wet weather, holding the ripe pollen safe and dry inside. When conditions become warm and dry the anthers crack open and the pollen spills out. As the earth warms up on sunny mornings during the growing season, many anthers begin to release their pollens. This is why hay fever sufferers are told to stay indoors in the early morning hours of bright spring and summer days.

Grains of dry, powdery pollen are sometimes carried enormous distances by the wind. They have been collected from the air in the middle of the Atlantic Ocean and at nineteen thousand feet above the Mississippi River. But long-distance travel is the exception. Most airborne pollen falls within a few feet of the plant producing it.

Not all blowing pollen causes hay fever. Most kinds of wind-pollinated plants give off too little pollen to matter because the plants themselves are not very numerous. Some species may flood the air with powder but cause little distress because their pollen is not very irritating. Pine trees, for example, shed a heavy blanket of yellow powder over their surroundings, but they are not an important cause of hay fever.

Most plants flower for a fairly short period of time. The exact blooming dates for each species vary with location. In the southern parts of the United States, flowers open earlier and blossoms last longer than in the North.

In most parts of the United States and Canada, three major groups of hay fever plants come into flower each year in regular order. The first are the trees and bushes. Next to flower are the grasses. And finally, rounding off the hay fever year, come the dreaded weedy plants.

TWO

THE FIRST WAVE:
POLLEN FROM TREES
AND BUSHES

Most wind-pollinated trees and bushes flower in early spring before their leaves come out or are fully grown. Flowers on naked branches are more fully exposed to the wind, and pollen is also less likely to be wasted by landing on nearby leaves.

A tree or a bush in your backyard doesn't always burst into flower on the same date each year. Warm, dry weather will bring earlier blooming. Coolness and rain may delay flowering for a week or two.

The amount of pollen given off by each of these plants also changes from year to year. Since their flower buds are formed during the previous spring and summer, the number will depend on growing conditions during that past year. But even with an abundant crop of flower buds, the quantity of pollen actually released when spring arrives may be low. Long periods of heavy rain can cause the plant to drop many of its unopened buds. A late heavy frost may freeze the buds and kill them.

A warm, dry spring is ideal for the release of pollen but bad news for hay fever sufferers.

Any plant that sends much pollen into the air may bother some sensitive people. But most early-spring hay fever is caused by a fairly small number of species.

Botanists organize the thousands of plant species into groups called plant families. Members of the same family share some important structures and appear to be closely related. Just as allergies run in human families, allergens tend to run in plant families. Because of this, people who are bothered by pollen from one plant often react in the same way to the pollen of other plant family members. Most of the trees and bushes that cause hay fever belong to these eight plant families.

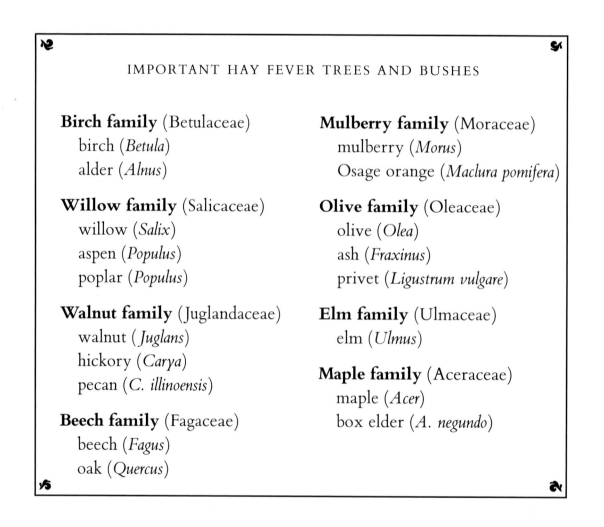

IMPORTANT HAY FEVER TREES AND BUSHES

Birch family (Betulaceae)
  birch (*Betula*)
  alder (*Alnus*)

Willow family (Salicaceae)
  willow (*Salix*)
  aspen (*Populus*)
  poplar (*Populus*)

Walnut family (Juglandaceae)
  walnut (*Juglans*)
  hickory (*Carya*)
  pecan (*C. illinoensis*)

Beech family (Fagaceae)
  beech (*Fagus*)
  oak (*Quercus*)

Mulberry family (Moraceae)
  mulberry (*Morus*)
  Osage orange (*Maclura pomifera*)

Olive family (Oleaceae)
  olive (*Olea*)
  ash (*Fraxinus*)
  privet (*Ligustrum vulgare*)

Elm family (Ulmaceae)
  elm (*Ulmus*)

Maple family (Aceraceae)
  maple (*Acer*)
  box elder (*A. negundo*)

The birch, willow, walnut, and beech families all have trees whose flowers grow crowded on a spike. Because it looks something like a cat's tail, this kind of flower spike is called a catkin.

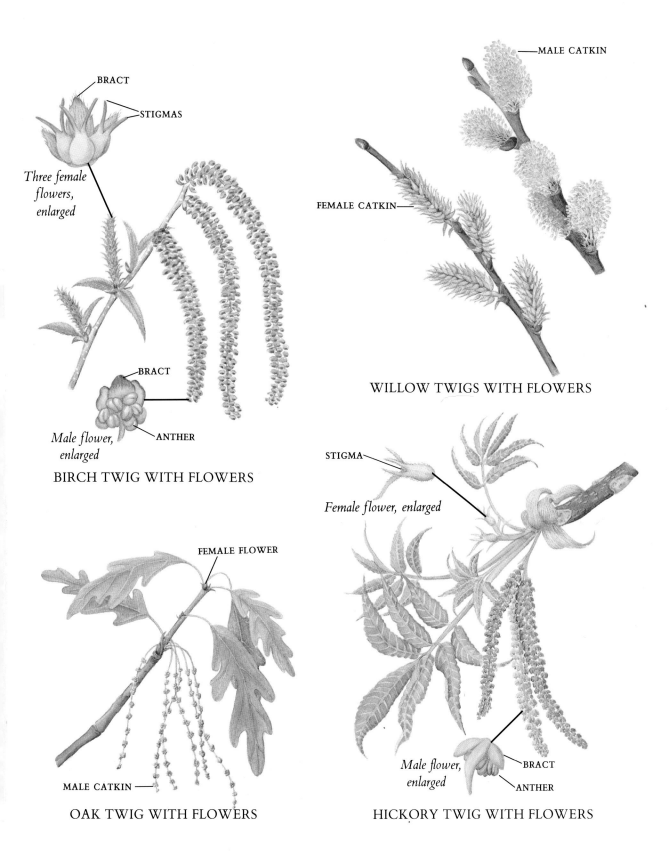

BRACT

STIGMAS

Three female flowers, enlarged

MALE CATKIN

FEMALE CATKIN

BRACT

ANTHER

Male flower, enlarged

BIRCH TWIG WITH FLOWERS

WILLOW TWIGS WITH FLOWERS

FEMALE FLOWER

STIGMA

Female flower, enlarged

MALE CATKIN

OAK TWIG WITH FLOWERS

Male flower, enlarged

BRACT

ANTHER

HICKORY TWIG WITH FLOWERS

Each catkin on a birch tree holds hundreds of tiny flowers. In spring, the catkins stretch out and dangle loosely in the breeze. Alder bushes are in the same family. Their catkins are similar and, like all members of the birch family, are wind-pollinated. Both birches and alders are common in many areas, and most hay fever caused by this family is due to them.

Willows are pollinated by insects. Their flowers have nectar and are sweet smelling and attract swarms of bees. But willow catkins look just like wind-pollinated flowers and their stamens produce lightweight pollen in great amounts. Some willow pollen is picked up and spread by the wind. Aspens and poplars, also in the willow family, produce even more pollen than willows. Their flowers have no nectar or perfume and are entirely wind-pollinated. Hay fever victims may be bothered by pollen from any of the trees in this family.

Walnut, hickory, and pecan trees, all in the walnut family, have large pollen grains that don't travel very far. But they do shed heavily, and where many grow together, as in an orchard, they may cause an allergy.

Although wind-pollinated, beech trees are not considered to be very troublesome. Oaks, in the same family, are a different story. About sixty different species of oak trees grow throughout North America, shedding vast amounts of pollen. They are major allergy plants.

Most members of the mulberry family growing in North America are wind-pollinated. White mulberry, also with flowers in catkins, was introduced from Asia in the hope of starting a silk industry. Its leaves are the main food of silkworms. Silk production failed but the tree flourished. It spread quickly, and in many places it is more common than the native red mulberry. Osage orange, in the same family, has male flowers clustered in small pom-poms rather than catkins. Osage orange originally grew only in Oklahoma, Arkansas, and Texas. Before barbed wire came into common use, it was planted as a living hedge on farms throughout the Northeast and Middle West. Like white mulberry, it has taken hold and spread in the areas where it was introduced.

The flowers of ashes, elms, and maples all hang in clusters.

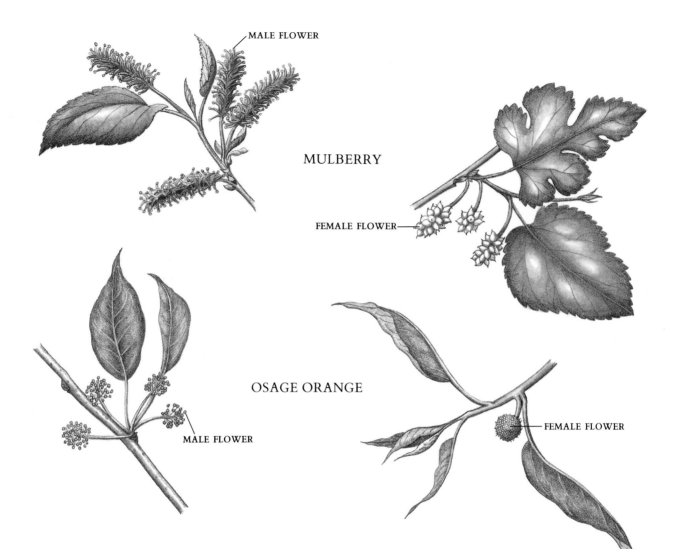

MALE FLOWER

MULBERRY

FEMALE FLOWER

OSAGE ORANGE

MALE FLOWER

FEMALE FLOWER

Ashes are the only plants in the olive family that depend on wind for pollination, but any member of the family may cause hay fever. Olive trees are grown in the southwestern United States, and privet bushes, in the same family, are common hedge plants everywhere. Although both have flowers that attract insects, some of their pollen also escapes into the air.

Some species of native elm bloom in the fall rather than the spring. Any elm may cause hay fever. The spring-flowering American elm was once the most familiar street tree in cities and towns throughout the United States. Vast numbers of this species have been killed by Dutch elm disease, making American elms less troublesome as hay fever plants.

17

ASH TWIG WITH MALE FLOWERS

ELM TWIG WITH FLOWERS

Flower, enlarged

STAMEN

PISTIL

Typical Maple Leaf
(Sugar Maple)

Box Elder Leaf

BOX ELDER TWIG
WITH MALE FLOWERS

Maple trees also lose some pollen to the air, but their flowers are usually insect-pollinated—with one exception. Box elder is the only maple that depends entirely on wind for pollination. It is also the only maple with leaflets instead of a single broad leaf. Each box elder leaf has three to seven small leaflets attached to a stalk. Box elder is a riverbank tree but it also grows around dumps, parking lots, and in other places where the ground has been disturbed. It is found in many parts of the United States and southern Canada. Wherever it is common, it is an important hay fever plant.

Most of the other trees with powerful allergens grow in smaller areas than the widespread plants described here. Some cypress and juniper species found only in parts of the southwestern United States cause strong reactions. The southernmost parts of the United States have some troublesome plants that survive only in very warm climates. One of these is the so-called Australian pine brought from Asia and Australia and planted in Florida and California. It spreads easily in those warm climates and has become a nuisance, crowding out native trees and adding more hay fever allergens to the air.

Arizona was once thought of as a paradise for hay fever sufferers. Today, pollen from introduced plants clouds the air in some parts of that state. As the population there surged in recent years, newcomers surrounded their houses with plantings of olive, privet, white mulberry, and cypress. As a result, pollen counts grew about ten times in twenty years. Now the number of hay fever cases in cities such as Tucson is well above the national average.

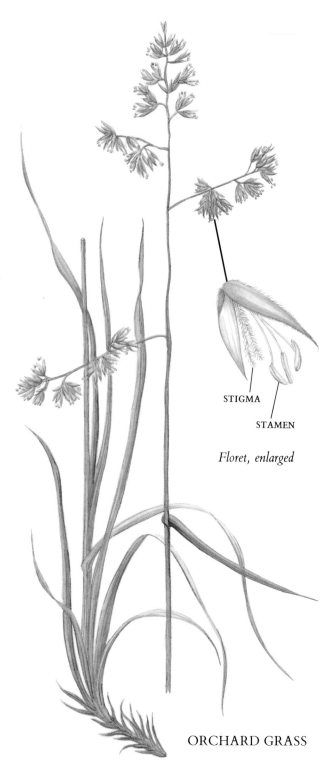

STIGMA

STAMEN

Floret, enlarged

ORCHARD GRASS

THREE
THE
GRASSES

It is hard for most people to think of grasses as plants with flowers. Grass flowers are so small that you sometimes need a magnifying glass just to see that they are in bloom.

Like the wind-pollinated tree flowers, grass flowers have no sepals or petals. But unlike most of the trees, their male and female parts usually grow side by side. A tiny grass flower, called a floret, usually has three stamens and two feathery stigmas.

Warm spring weather may cause grasses to release their pollen earlier than usual, and rain may delay it. But grass-flowering dates are fairly regular. Compared to the woody plants, grasses are less influenced by weather conditions.

The great majority of all grass

species are pollinated by wind. Grass pollen has some powerful allergens and causes more hay fever than does the pollen of flowering trees and bushes. Even worse, the pollens of different species of grass often contain some of the same allergens. So a person bothered by one kind of grass pollen is almost certain to be allergic to other species as well. Since over twelve hundred different kinds of grasses grow in North America, it would seem that there is no escape for the hay fever sufferer.

In fact, only a handful of grass species are important hay fever plants. Many native grasses on the American prairies grow in large colonies. Because they need only a little pollen to reach a neighboring plant, most of these prairie grasses do not shed heavily. In addition, some grass species that do give off a lot of pollen are simply too few in number to cause problems.

The seven most troublesome grasses are plants from Europe, Asia, and Africa that were introduced into North America. Some came with the colonists, and others were brought over in the early nineteenth century. With one exception, they are useful agricultural plants. But all seven produce much irritating pollen, and all of them have spread far beyond the borders of farmers' fields. They thrive on roadsides, vacant lots, and other places where the ground has been disturbed.

In the warmest parts of the United States, grass flowering is almost nonstop, with some plants shedding pollen from February to December. For most of the country, the main part of the season comes in early summer. Because the release of airborne grass pollen often peaks during the weeks when roses are blooming, hay fever that comes in late spring and early summer is sometimes called rose fever. People *can* get hay fever from rose pollen. But since roses are pollinated by insects, only a little rose pollen is likely to be picked up by the wind. You would probably have to live among the roses or sniff the blossoms to get a heavy dose.

In eastern North America and along the West Coast, the season for grass hay fever begins in spring with the flowering of sweet vernal grass. It grows in fields, meadows, and along roadsides. Unlike the other major hay fever grasses, it has no value as a food for grazing animals.

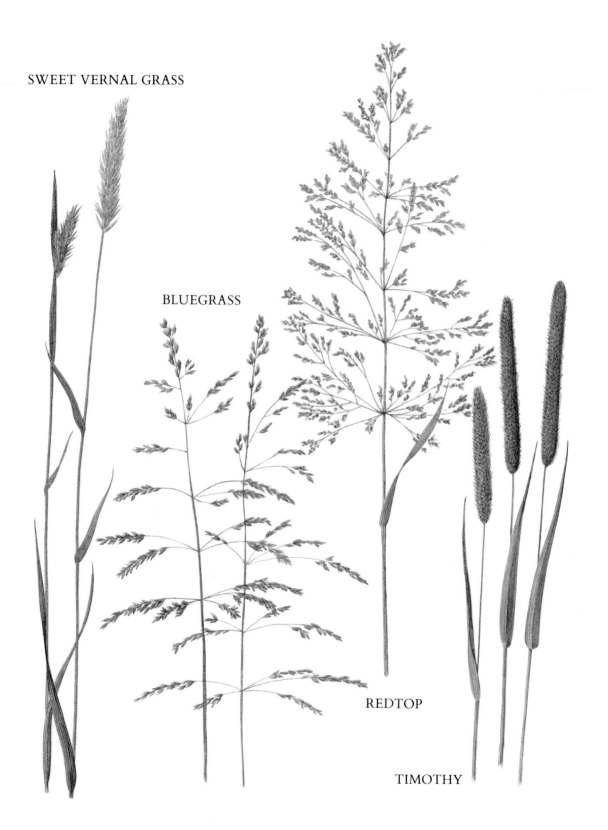

SWEET VERNAL GRASS

BLUEGRASS

REDTOP

TIMOTHY

Orchard grass and the bluegrasses, grown throughout the United States and southern Canada, also bloom early. Orchard grass is cultivated in pastures and hay fields. Because it can grow in shade, it is also planted between rows of trees in orchards. Several species of bluegrass contribute to the pollen load. They are important animal food and some, such as Kentucky bluegrass, are also widely planted in lawns.

The redtop grasses and timothy flower throughout the summer. Together they cause most late-season grass hay fever in the United States. Both are grown for animal feed, and one species of redtop, called creeping bent grass, is also used for turf and lawns.

Johnson grass and Bermuda grass flourish in the South, where they may be in flower for most months of the year. Both are cultivated in pastures. Johnson grass often invades agricultural fields, and Bermuda grass is also used as a lawn grass. Bermuda grass is blamed for ten to twenty percent of the pollen in Tucson's air. Even if it is mowed, its flowers may grow so close to the ground that the lawn mower blade misses them.

These seven major offenders are certainly not the only grasses that

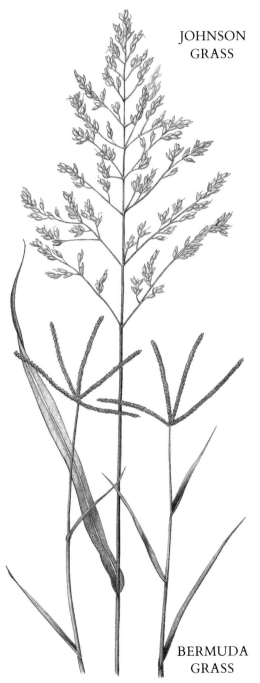

JOHNSON GRASS

BERMUDA GRASS

contribute to hay fever. A few native species do as well. Among them are the various grama grasses, which provide valuable animal food in western grazing areas.

Most of the others known to cause hay fever—brome grasses, fescues, rye grasses, and velvet grass—were brought from Europe and Asia. They are planted for forage, for hay, or in lawn-seed mixes. Like orchard grass and the other introduced forage grasses, they tend to escape from the places where they are wanted. Their seeds scatter and find a foothold in any disturbed bit of ground where they land—roadsides, old fields, vacant lots, and cracks in the pavement.

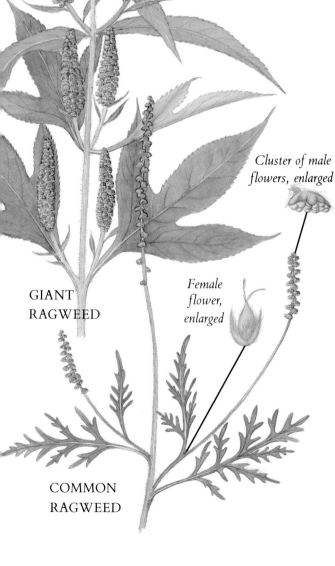

GIANT
RAGWEED

COMMON
RAGWEED

*Cluster of male
flowers, enlarged*

*Female
flower,
enlarged*

FOUR

THE
WEEDS

Many different kinds of weeds have airborne pollen that may cause hay fever. As with the trees and shrubs, most belong to just a few plant families.

In contrast to the grasses, the weeds causing most allergic reactions are native to America. Ragweeds are easily the most troublesome of all the hay fever plants in North America. They grow in each of the lower forty-eight states and in Mexico and southern Canada.

Ragweeds and most of the other hay fever weeds are pioneers that take over disturbed soil. They thrive in neglected places where the original plant growth has been removed or injured—on roadsides, in empty lots, and in abandoned fields. Before

Europeans settled the continent, ragweeds grew mainly in ground that had been disturbed by natural forces: on riverbanks washed clean by high water or on prairie sod scraped bare by the hooves of buffaloes. As forests were cleared and the land plowed, vast new areas were opened for the spread of weeds.

Giant and common ragweed are the most widespread of the seventeen different ragweed species. Their numerous male flowers hang down from a central spike and may produce as many as a billion pollen grains on a single plant. They release most of their pollen in the morning hours of warm, dry days in the late summer. The female flowers, tucked in at the bases of the upper leaves, are far fewer.

Ragweed flowering is linked to the seasonal movements of the sun. The blossoms begin to open as summer days become shorter and the nights longer. In any particular location, therefore, the ragweed season always begins and ends at the same time each year. In most places, the plants flower for four to six weeks, from about the middle of July until September. Under bright city streetlights, however, they may continue to bloom and release pollen until late September.

Ragweeds belong to a huge family of plants called the composite or aster family. While most of the family is pollinated by insects, many of the wind-pollinated members are known to cause hay fever. Marsh elders, in the same family, are closely related to ragweeds and similar in appearance, and they share some of the same allergens. Various species of marsh elder grow along the Atlantic and Gulf coasts and are common in the West from Oklahoma to Utah.

Next to ragweeds, the most

MARSH ELDER

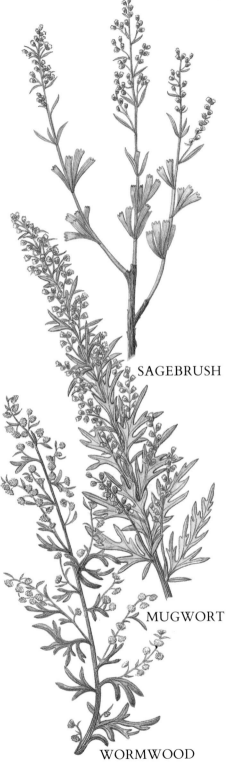

SAGEBRUSH

MUGWORT

WORMWOOD

important hay fever weeds belong to a large genus of plants in the composite family named *Artemisia*. Although these plants are found coast-to-coast, they are most common on the dry plains and high deserts of the American West. Sagebrush, mugwort, and wormwood are some of the common names for the many species of *Artemisia*. Their tiny flowers are clustered along the stems and release heavy loads of pollen. Their stems and leaves are often fragrant but bitter to the taste. Cattle on overgrazed western ranges eat all the better-tasting species and leave *Artemisia* to multiply without competition.

Goldenrods, also in the composite family, have long been blamed for hay fever, even though they are pollinated by insects. Most species shed only small amounts of pollen, and little of it gets into the air. But someone who is sensitive to ragweed is also likely to be allergic to goldenrods, dandelions, marigolds, or any other composite. Some people even have allergic reactions when they eat sunflower seeds or honey that was made from the pollen of composite flowers.

Both the goosefoot and amaranth families contain many bothersome species. These two families are so closely related that their pollens look alike and carry the same allergens.

The goosefoot family includes common weeds such as lamb's-quarters, which grows coast-to-coast, as well as spinach and beet plants. Spinach and beets are usually harvested before the plants produce any flowers.

SOME WEEDS IN THE GOOSEFOOT FAMILY

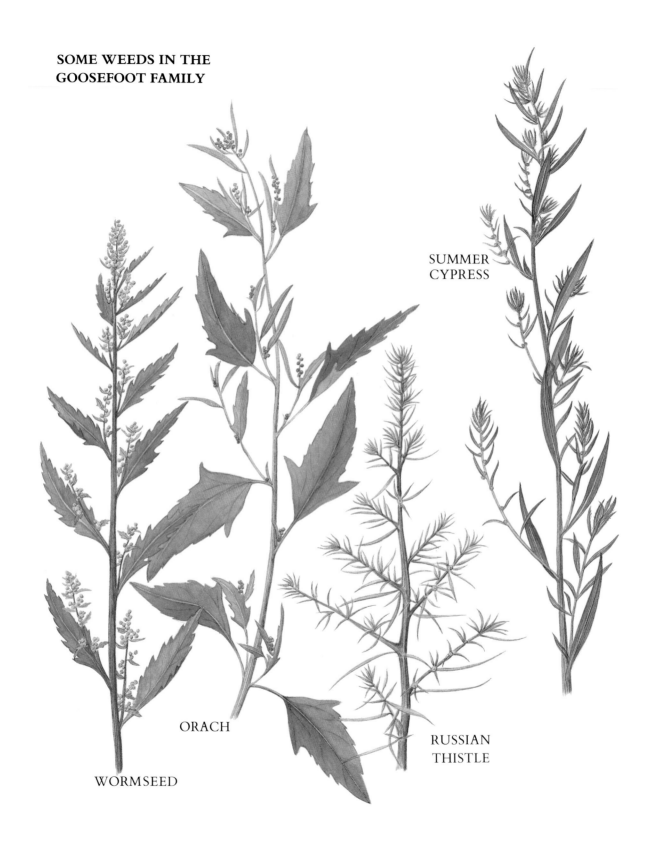

SUMMER
CYPRESS

ORACH

RUSSIAN
THISTLE

WORMSEED

As a cause of hay fever, the goosefoot family is most troublesome in the western half of North America. Many goosefoot weeds thrive on the dry plains where the soil is high in salts. Dozens of species with common names such as saltbush, summer cypress, wormseed, and orach cause hay fever wherever they are numerous. The plant called Russian thistle is an imported weed that is common in the West and increasing in the East. Old plant parts from the Russian thistle break off and become tumbleweeds that roll across the fields and spread the seeds. Its pollen contains powerful allergens.

Hay fever weeds in the amaranth family are amaranth, pigweed, and water hemp. Creeping amaranth (also called prostrate pigweed) and redroot amaranth (also called rough pigweed) are two species that grow coast-to-coast.

REDROOT AMARANTH

CREEPING AMARANTH

While most hay fever weeds reach their flowering peaks in late summer, some give off large amounts of pollen earlier in the season. English plantain, in the plantain family, releases pollen from early summer until late fall. This common lawn weed also takes hold in old fields, waste places, and any kind of open area. It sheds large amounts of pollen and is a powerful source of hay fever in some areas.

Sheep sorrel, in the buckwheat family, is an introduced weed. It is found coast-to-coast in abandoned farm fields and pastures. It often forms large colonies and may flower in spring and for most of the summer.

Most of the other weedy hay fever plants are important only locally, where special conditions favor large populations of a species. Fireweed, for example, is a common wildflower in the North, where it springs up on land that was recently burned or cleared. Although the flowers are insect-pollinated, small amounts of pollen are picked up by the wind. Some loggers in the Northwest, working among thick stands of flowering fireweed, have become sensitive to its pollen.

Fireweed is one of the very few hay fever plants with bright, attractive flowers. Almost all of the other weedy species are dull-looking plants. No one would give them a second look—except a botanist or an educated victim of hay fever. And no one will be annoyed if the hay fever sufferer, acting in self-defense, bends over and pulls the weed out of the ground.

SHEEP SORREL

AVOIDING HAY FEVER POLLEN

The best way to manage hay fever is to avoid the pollens that cause the allergy.

- Identify the cause of your hay fever by observing which hay fever plants are flowering when your symptoms appear. Try to stay away from places where these plants bloom.
- Some pollen sources can be controlled: Keep grass cut short to prevent flowering and remove wind-pollinated weeds.
- On warm, dry days during the hay fever season, try to avoid morning activities in the outdoors.
- Keep house and car windows closed.
- Use an air conditioner with filters that remove small particles from the air.
- Any soft surface that is outdoors will pick up pollen from the air: outdoor clothing, laundry hung out to dry, your pet's fur. Be aware of these sources and avoid those you can. Frequent washing will remove pollen from your own hair.

BOOKS ABOUT HAY FEVER PLANTS

Jelks, Mary. *Allergy Plants*. Tampa, Fla.: World-Wide Publications, 1986. Very brief descriptions and excellent color photographs of many plants.

Lewis, Walter H., Prathibha Vinay, and Vincent E. Zenger. *Airborne and Allergenic Pollen of North America*. Baltimore: Johns Hopkins University Press, 1983. A book written for doctors who treat allergy, this contains more detailed plant descriptions than the Jelks book. Black-and-white photographs of the plants and maps showing the areas where they grow.

INDEX

Illustrations are in **boldface**.